DEAR EDITOR

ALSO BY AMY NEWMAN

Camera Lyrica

fall

Order, or Disorder

Dear Editor

AMY NEWMAN

Winner of the 2011
Lexi Rudnitsky Editor's Choice Award

A Karen & Michael Braziller Book

PERSEA BOOKS / NEW YORK

Persea Books, Inc.
277 Broadway
New York, NY 10007

Library of Congress Cataloging-in-Publication Data
Newman, Amy (Amy Lynn)
Dear editor / Amy Newman.
        p. cm.
"A Karen & Michael Braziller book."
ISBN 978-0-89255-387-7 (original trade pbk. : alk. paper)
I. Title.
PS3564.E9148D43 2011
813'.54—dc23

                                2011030272

Designed by Rita Lascaro
First Edition

Printed in the United States of America

Contents

Is this, sir, what you asked me to tell you?

— EMILY DICKINSON

DEAR EDITOR

Fall

3 October

Dear Editor:

Please consider the enclosed poems for
publication. They are from my manuscript,
X = Pawn Capture, a lyrical study of a particular
kind of chess game played within my family:
the first move has to be made by someone who
doesn't understand the basic rules. My grandmother
didn't like this game, and usually, when the wind,
drifting as it did by the kitchen as she baked,
brought something in as if a gift, something like
berry scent or that of the sweet mixed grasses, she
would lean out with a smile as if remembering
a saint, one she knew personally, one she took
personally. *Which saint?* I'd ask, and she would
make it up: *Saint Berry*, she'd say, picking up a rook
and swishing it around the board. *Saint Berry, who
protested the loss of her virginity by heaping ash and
kindling on the dinner of her betrayer.* She'd move
the piece in the air and place it somewhere on a
white square. *All right old man, you got your way.*
And later there'd be cabbages in red sauce and a
half glass of wine.

Thank you for your consideration, and for
reading. I have enclosed an SASE, and look forward
to hearing from you.

Sincerely,
Amy Newman

Dear Editor:

Please consider the enclosed poems for publication. They are from my manuscript, *X = Pawn Capture*, a lyrical study of chess. I had a family love for chess, a game my grandfather once insisted that young children should never play, because of the obvious difficulties. I don't think he meant it at the time, but as I was a child, it confused me a little, with him setting up the board and clacking the queens midair, saying: *Let's play!* Perhaps he was trying to make me laugh, as he did when I was so little—should I say as "little as *something*," make that vivid? And I stood on his hands in the air like a chess piece, and he raised me up like—should I say "Icarus"? But the workshop said: *avoid myth at all costs because it's too cliché.* And in workshop, the readers always want to know: What color was the room? Did my grandfather really smoke while he bathed? Did our horse really run away that day, and if that was true, why in the second stanza do I picture the horse out the window, after she'd fled, after my grandfather warned me: *Don't throw the ashes near the horse's feed*? My grandfather warned me about a lot of mistakes, and I made them anyway. The horse might not have been at the window, but when I think of her there, I think of something inexpressible.

Thank you for your consideration, and for reading. I have enclosed an SASE, and look forward to hearing from you.

Sincerely,
Amy Newman

Dear Editor:

Please consider the enclosed poems for publication. They are from my manuscript, *X = Pawn Capture*, a lyrical study of a particular kind of chess game one played when one played chess in my family: the opening move had to be made by someone who didn't like to play. When my grandmother first married my grandfather, there were no notions of spilled chess pieces or afternoons filled only with a violin's questioning and the scratch of a stiff rook on a black square. She had imagined if she wrote out wedding invitations to her favorite saints they might show, to give a blessing. So there are somewhere yellowed invitations to Bernard of Clairvaux (whether for the bees or the wax with which he is associated she never said) and her favorite, Saint Lucy, who was so pure that God granted her immobility when the Romans tried to move her to a brothel; this would have appealed to my grandmother for the obvious reasons.

I once asked what had happened when her saints did not materialize on the wedding day, and she took a rook from the chessboard and shook it like a bean in her hands. *Who says that? Lucy came in and winked behind the altar, stuck out her tongue at your grandfather, and since then my vision is crisp*

and private. Asked about Bernard of Clairvaux,
she kind of sighed and got back to fussing with the
dinner towels. Men, I got the impression, were a
mystery to her, saint or otherwise.

Thank you for your consideration, and for
reading. I have enclosed an SASE, and look forward
to hearing from you.

Sincerely,
Amy Newman

Dear Editor:

Please consider the enclosed poems for
publication. They are from my manuscript,
$X = Pawn\ Capture$, a lyrical study of chess
I am writing as a response assignment. The
teacher said, *Write what you know,* and I thought
if I had to do that, I would cry instead and miss
out on the workshop discussion. Here's what
I know: I know that my grandfather thought I
was foolish, that my belly ached for no reason.
And that when I brought out the chess pieces,
and tried to polish them, it was a distraction
from being a child, I was wasting some good
afternoons. Why didn't I want to play like the
others, awash in their apple trees, their berry
bush bowls, and their bicycle races? Isolation
rang in my abdomen like a sliver of ash in an
eye. I clung to my grandmother's skirts and cried.
The doctor came in a white stiff coat, and took
the appendix out. My family stood around and
waited, and when I woke up, my grandfather's
body, whiter than I could imagine, drifted close
to the ceiling in fumes like a story about ether-
soaked cotton. But the needles were sleek and
polished, pure silver. I wish chess were clean,
and free of distortion. And the words for that
are in your dictionary.

Thank you for your consideration, and for reading. I have enclosed an SASE, and look forward to hearing from you.

Sincerely,

Amy Newman

Dear Editor:

Please consider the enclosed poems for
publication. They are from my manuscript,
$X = Pawn Capture$, a series of poems about chess
and, in particular, about the spectacular queen,
which has the combined moves of the rook and
the bishop. When I dream the queen's moves on
a grassy board, she splays out in a sunburst and
points like a compass and the flies and the gnats
ring her crown points. And the queen must be
pretty to distract the opponent, and must acquiesce
when I ask her to move. And I must watch the board
for any secrets or hint of trouble. For the path of
the thoughtful child shall not enter the land of the
dread lion without a tool kit made from animal
hide, leathers of words and vast support, winged
creatures, sailors who eat ash as an appetizer. My
grandmother says the saints don't want me to sleep,
they want me up and ringing the sunlight, and
bringing in berries from the bright torrid bushes,
and playing with the other children, even though
those children move around in indistinct circles and
hash patterns that I find difficult to read. I hope
your magazine uses words from the dictionary, and
places them in the orderly rows that permit them to
see each other only to the extent that they need to.
I needn't remind an editor that unlike the queen on

a white or black square, most letters in the alphabet may not move diagonally.

Thank you for your consideration, and for reading. I have enclosed an SASE, and look forward to hearing from you.

Sincerely,
Amy Newman

15 October

Dear Editor:

This morning when I went out to collect the
leaves from the back deck, the slope of the yard was
unconvincing and nameless. How am I supposed to
know enough to make something happen on a page
that will convince me of anything? And then a red-
tailed hawk creased the eye's vision and startled
a show of darkish squirrels who were hunting
acorns the big tree had lost from its moorings of
fantail leaves. And the world parted its curtains, its
scratchy and difficult weave, and a deer entered
from stage left. Everything could have been still,
and remained still, under a blank page of cloud
and above the random field of unconcern that is
where I live, and I would yet be there absorbing the
about-to-happen, until I wrestled in my head with
presentation, and the deer noticed my breathing;
a pinioned ear swung brown cones and dials and
the curtains began their snap shut. But the deer's
coat glossed like a television, and a kind of word
appeared on its side, some series of symbols I could
have used to tell you. My mechanisms clacked
and bent but the pattern on the brown body didn't
speak in our easy and flattened alphabet. Instead,
it showed glare and depth, something dimensional
and respiratory, with music and a story behind it,
the etymology of person meeting deer, it maintained

several possibilities at once, and sustained—if I had
had a Motorola V620© phone with Integrated 300K
camera with 4X zoom at the ready, the poem about
the world could have been taken as it was rendered
in that deer's word-like body. Whatever it knew
and showed in creamy gloss I could not cipher or
translate or hold. It swifted with something like fear
or disdain into the back of the world behind the
house.

   Thank you for your consideration, and for
reading. I have enclosed an SASE, and look forward
to hearing from you.

Sincerely,
Amy Newman

Dear Editor:

Please consider the enclosed poems for
publication. They are from my manuscript,
X = Pawn Capture. I picture the chessboard as the
field on which my grandparents first made love,
and atop this, the series of black and white squares
represent their commitments and arguments and
unholy sacrifices for the children who will never
live up to their hopes: the chess pieces are the
grandchildren who further disappoint them. For
the time the board is actively telling the story of
their meeting, like cinema, it flashes with trees and
words, subtitles which I am imagining entirely. And
my grandmother's dress opens to its inside lining,
against which the projector shows her when she is
young, and opening again her dress, and inside that
dress the dark lands of her upbringing, with, if you
look into my head, into my imagination, tiny figures
approaching who will not be friendly.

Every pawn move on the board creates
some kind of weakness, and as she grows into
womanhood I can only envision (by combining her
songs with the food she cooks) what she remembers
of this crucial teenage time: a wallpapered part of
the parlor with a portrait of a Lord with an open
chest and a flaming heart. It must be October
17th, when Margaret Mary Alacoque saw the heart

in fire and grace that made her a saint, a pretty
saint who is always represented by her dark habit
fluttering and the Heart of the Almighty afire. My
grandmother remembers that when first she saw
my grandfather, somewhat fine in his knee boots
and carrying a rucksack of grain, approaching from
across the hill, his shirt was half torn from some
argument. It kindled a typical want or desire that a
human understands as love but if she were a saint,
my grandmother would have seen right through this
phony vision and sent the mortal packing.

Thank you for your consideration, and for
reading. I have enclosed an SASE, and look forward
to hearing from you.

Sincerely,
Amy Newman

2 November

Dear Editor:

Please consider the enclosed poems for
publication. They are from my manuscript
X = Pawn Capture, an in-depth study of something
I pretend to lyricize: my grandfather's love for chess
and how it ruined my grandmother's afternoons
and evenings.

I loved the scent of her cooking as the deer
wandered by our wintery windows in our Russian-
like town of upstate New York by the Finger Lakes
region, such as it was. My grandmother believed
that even her saints wouldn't deign to visit in this
white, blank, and unreligious cul-de-sac, imagined
they wouldn't find the strength or perhaps desire to
back their wheelish wagons of grace up to the pale
siding off the garage. So when the outside world
seemed so unfortunate in its whites and frozen
apologies of snow, she'd boil water for Wissotzky
tea and open the calendar to pick a saint, whistling
along with the kettle. In the next room I'd scrape a
knight in a fancy way and listen for the hot water to
stir and then annoy the bottom of the metal kettle. If
there were parents telling stories to children, those
tales would have been encouraging in that frosted
landscape: rich lions and Indian princesses. As my
grandfather flicked ash into the flat base of the
glass dish and watched the window, I thought, right

now a little tormented girl is being beaten for her belief, rippling with fervor so she doesn't mind, and she's risen and become dimensional on a plastic card, flattered in twisted ropes of framing golds and uninterested in worldly things. This I could conjure for a playmate.

Thank you for your consideration, and for reading. I have enclosed an SASE, and look forward to hearing from you.

Sincerely,
Amy Newman

Dear Editor:

Please consider the enclosed poems for
publication. They are from my manuscript
X = *Pawn Capture*, a lyrical exploration of chess
moves and the desire to know the world's inner
workings in a language unencumbered by doubts.
The patron saint of chess is considered by many to
be Theresa of Avila, but recent scholarship disputes
this and instead considers the possibility that
chess is a trick my own grandfather played on me
while my grandmother cried in the kitchen into an
apron I myself have invented for the purposes of
this story. For when that pretty and agonized Saint
Theresa saw the Sacred, He showed Himself to her
in flecks and hints, a leg here, an arm there, the holy
hokey pokey where my doubt is never completely
satisfied. As far as I'm concerned, Theresa might
have had a better chance of convincing the doubters
if she had on her person at the time a Nokia 3650
Phone© with video playback, because evidence is
everything, though then of course there would be
those who said the whole series was photoshopped.
But still. I would have loved to have seen it. And
maybe to know for certain would eliminate doubt
or wonder, and would have explained the look on
my grandmother's face when my grandfather came
in the house with evasion and something I want to

describe but cannot. Because it is not our privilege to understand the world, which is shown to us in such irritating dimensions and swatches, like the scratchy tweeds I would have preferred to the wrinkled handkerchiefs of my upbringing.

Thank you for your consideration, and for reading. I have enclosed an SASE, and look forward to hearing from you.

Sincerely,
Amy Newman

Dear Editor:

Please consider these poems for publication.
They are from my manuscript X = *Pawn Capture*,
a lyrical study of the effect of chess on my
grandparents' marriage, if you can call it that. But
no more whining.

Chess is a game of skill, and I watched the
afternoon sun wash the cells from my arms as
I moved the pawn in a diagonal, waiting for the
sound of something coming to a boil in the kitchen.
When water starts thinking in the pot it erases what
it thought before the boil: that's the trouble with
childhood and whatever I was told to remember. But
this has to be important: my aunt fixing a cigarette
as it bent away from her, my uncle staring moodily
out the window, remembering perhaps how he'd
accepted the sum of $7,500.00 from my grandfather
to marry my aunt because they shared a faith, and
she was in love with the Italian fellow, and would
have gone off the rails in love and never returned,
in love; something I can't write about flashing
through my aunt's eyes, something made of a
creamy thought, a one-dimensional flat and creamy
idea. My grandmother called her to the calendar
to discuss the female saints, and they settled on
Panacea, without a trace of irony as far as I could
tell. It must have been the first of May.

But what if it had been the 15th of October?
That's the day of Theresa of Avila, the pretty girl
with all the troubles who ran away to see the lord in
the first show of fast-frame shots we now know as
the quick cuts of MTV: arm, heart, lung, cornea, arm
bone and digestive tract, oh holy saint of grace who
like my aunt understood only in pieces; she would
have watched for you for hours on that Sunday
afternoon as the men puffed ash and moved plastic
ideas around in circles. Whatever gestures that you
made by coming into the heart of the suffering I
imagine was patterning in the white and partial bits
of tree and lake that gave itself up through the snow.
The family hung on until we twisted out the evening
light, and I wonder if that night while she slept,
my aunt saw your vision like a shower of ideas,
and curled under her blanket, thinking of specific
fleshy pieces her Italian had shown her, as a way of
revealing his love. That would be pretty for her.

Thank you for your consideration, and for
reading. I have enclosed an SASE, and look forward
to hearing from you.

Sincerely,
Amy Newman

Dear Editor:

I can remember in high school, when a boy
I knew only slightly would take me for a walk
and put an awkward arm in a hug position on my
waist, and pull in, tug at what I was. As I moved
past the constellations in the outer part of my eye,
I would see the face of the boy and think of how
in Mitchell's translation of Rilke, *every angel is
terrifying*. But I hadn't known the biography yet, so
I thought of them, Rainer and Clara, holding each
other and wondering at the tether of the angelic
as it accosted them. I imagined love and dreamed
in girlish circles of a twining. Returning to the
real, I would see the boy's face sour with what he
perceived to be my failure at assuming him. When
he kissed me I was thinking of how ink is absorbed
so prettily into paper fiber, and imagining how
books were sewn together at the seams. In such
periphery I laid my head.

So there went the high school years and so
many who wondered at my silences. I was weak,
I was so wrapped up in ideas. And now to think
of all that could have been in high school, the
traditions and the cheers, and the trim waists of
the slim footballers who ran and huffed so that the
town would be delighted. But the patron saint of our
high school was St. Brigid of Ireland, who should

have been a cheerleader for her beauty, for the way
she could never bear to see anyone sad or hungry,
and how the cows prospered under her care. And
out in that green field where the boys tried to take
me, there wanders my imagination, and there it
diminishes as I mature, as I come as the poet says
into the heart of suffering and leave behind the
stories that will not sustain me. As it should be, so
sayeth the texts. But there you are.

Thank you for your consideration, and for
reading. I have enclosed an SASE, and look forward
to hearing from you.

Sincerely,
Amy Newman

Dear Editor:

Please consider the enclosed poems for
publication. They are from my manuscript,
X = Pawn Capture, a manuscript about how
chess may be a metaphor, and in this case the
dry and silent intellectual play of the board acts
as the absence of my grandfather's desire. If my
grandmother gets to have a metaphor, I choose the
calendar that hung against the cellar door, and also,
her regarding it, humming a blurry song about the
path such sorrow took. During the winter of dried
grains and only a few berries she would share with
me her saints, who were splayed across the calendar
in fabulous stories, gleaming tresses under torture
and burning. Angela of Foligno stood on clouds as
she approached the Lord, having endured whatever
was her torment, and was a source of comfort for
those who suffer from temptation. Along with her
was Mary of Egypt, whose mortal end was like a
child's bedtime story: a peaceful lion to bury her
because she'd mended her ways. Whatever she had
done to bring the lion to this dry desert and out of
its slick jungle where I pictured it sleeping, I could
not tell. I imagine the lion had a long walk home
with its regal tail and its marvelous mane. Mary of
Egypt might have danced with men she didn't know
well, or kissed, as I have, football players from her

high school, without any real desire, because how embarrassing to have to say *no*. Although I wouldn't mention this to my grandparents, I understand such adolescent confusion, and sometimes when I am rich with regret I look out the windows for a beige, lumbering body or massive paw prints.

Sincerely,
Amy Newman

20 November

Dear Editor:

Please consider the enclosed poems for
publication. They are from my manuscript,
X = Pawn Capture, a lyrical study of the history of
chess as my grandfather misrepresented it to me
because he loved to tell his stories or, if you like
the sound of this better, because I was too young to
comprehend his indifference to me. In any case I
preferred more my grandmother's understanding
of a story, how her calendar was full of images
of needles and flames and rushes of wheat, all
standing for the way a young girl was left to fend
for herself when the Romans decided to make a
saint of her. We would sit in front of the stove while
something proceeded though its permutations
in order to be consumed by evening, and she'd
speak of Saint Panacea's stepmother, Margherita
di Locarno Sesia, who stabbed the little girl with
a spindle because she was so pure, and I would
imagine *Rapunzel, Rapunzel, let down your hair,* and
castles of stone hewn out of quarries and bright-
stepping horses with braided manes.
    While the ashy length of my grandfather's
cigar would measure the evening's disappointments
by increments, the part of my brain built for
learning and memory was focused on the strength
of the hair follicle required for a healthy man

to climb a high tower braced only by the golden
length of her hair. If I could have transferred these
thoughts to that part of the brain that processes
motivation and emotion, or reading or language,
I could write how Rapunzel felt as she supported
the king's son's weight up the tower, only partially
reeling from the stress on the outer root sheath
and the dermal papillae. And all the unhappiness
that follows in that story is because her mother, one
enchanted evening, was hungry for wild ferns.

Thank you for your consideration, and for
reading. I have enclosed an SASE, and look forward
to hearing from you.

Sincerely,
Amy Newman

Winter

Dear Editor:

Please consider the enclosed poems for
publication. They are from my manuscript,
X = Pawn Capture, an exploration of how my
grandfather used chess as a way to divert a child's
attention from the absence of love between her
grandparents and my attempts to capture in
language their magnificent silences, which could
have been visitations from ethereal beings for all
they told me.

The pawns on the chessboard are workers,
hard workers who get no thanks in this life, as my
grandfather would explain. That's why there are
more pawns than any other pieces, because life is
hard and tiring, and they suffer, and are sacrificed,
so that the community can continue and the game
can be played. I would like to see the knight protect
a pawn once in a while, especially a girl pawn, who
has let her hair down the long side of a castle and
allowed him to climb up its vermillion border. But
my grandfather tells me that a girl pawn would
be run out of town on a rail because she would
be nothing but trouble, a bee in the bonnet of the
community with her frills and her soft skins and
the hiding of the special areas, and the Queen, of
all pieces, would see to it that any young lady who
came calling even to remark *What a cold day we*

have! or *How are you doing kind sir?* would not last long, he might say while watching my grandmother peel from an eternal mound of onions one large and stubborn skin that unrolled only in bits and flakes.

But if the girl pawn *was* trapped in the castle piece and the knight watched her sighing, day after day, I think then that even the chokeberries that the birds devoured outside our windows on these cold days might instead stay in their first, pure, flowery blooms, so impressed the space outside our house would be by the atmosphere of real high school love, and not whatever it was that made the boy who was trying out for the football team stare from the corner of our street as I stumbled away like a spent insect after a curious and feeble forced embrace, lips entirely embarrassed and neck dismayed at his scratchy growth that assaulted, rearranging my shirts and skirts which were only pulled at a little, though when I got home and undressed in my room, my blouse would refuse to crumple in a heap that didn't look compromising. And outside my window no steadfast knight, who would rather die than force his hands down the open collar of my blouse and giggle while his knees pressed and pried like tweezers. No knight outside in the cold air awaiting with glistening eyes by the chokeberries,

sighing, or anyone interested in seeing if my hair,
now gleaming and yellow and strong as steel,
would lift them to some noble cause. In the kitchen
my grandmother tore at the spice leaves, and in
the main room my grandfather remained, forever
irritated at chess.

Thank you for your consideration, and for
reading. I have enclosed an SASE, and look forward
to hearing from you.

Sincerely,
Amy Newman

16 December

Dear Editor:

The one thing you have to understand is how
my grandmother's hand felt against my neck as
she discussed the merits of each individual saint
on those afternoons and evenings when the light
in the windows hesitated across the aspects of our
house. She has surprisingly delicate hands, after
all those rutabagas and cabbages and arguments
with the butcher about lean versus fat in the cow's
full body, and when she told me the stories of
martyrdom, the curve of her hand rested against the
wisps of my thin, useless hair. What is it about this
moment that compels me to write you? I wanted to
tell you about the intersection between her mortal
warmth and the stories of what she admired, such
as Saint Elizabeth Achler, Elisabeth the Good, who
fled from her troubling parents to live a pure life,
a religious life (the hand in patting motions on
my mortal head) and was subject to ecstasies (and
her hand rubs gently on my mortal neck). Of those
ecstasies my grandmother instructed me: a saint
would be in a state of suspension as she listened to
an inner birdsong of religious clacking and hawing,
and sometimes the saint would see others in her
inner circle as did Joan when Margaret of Antioch
came to her, having survived so many cruelties and
torments and insults and burnings and boilings,

and her little cross that irritated the inside of the
snake who swallowed her, and did she and Joan
gossip in their moment of recognition, hovering as
they did between Ideal Beings and the nonsense
of this world? How I loved to think that my own
experience might impress my grandmother. For as
you know, the ecstasies are for one who knows for
the moment what it is to be out of place with the
world, from the Greek *ek*, out; *histemi*, place, and I
could do that with my eyes closed.

Thank you for your consideration, and for
reading. I have enclosed an SASE, and look forward
to hearing from you.

Sincerely,
Amy Newman

Dear Editor:

Please consider the enclosed poems for
publication. They are from my manuscript,
X = Pawn Capture, an exploration of how attentive
I was versus how wily my grandparents were in
raising a tainted child. But if I *tell* you that, I will
have not *rendered*, which my workshop class says
is something I must do. When I think of the word
render I am reminded of how we get fat from our
animals and boil it for seasoning, to take from their
bodies the moist or succulent essence of them in
life and transfer it, as one uses a metaphor, on to the
pan or the onion or the bread. And when the bread
of the flesh is rendered unto me on Sundays as a
favor to my grandparents, I try not to think of Saint
Theresa who saw the Host only in the snapshots
and leftovers He provided, and how irritated she
must have been with her inability to get a clear
picture and maintain the dimensional Lord in
her apprehension of Him. Because how stubborn
of Him to make it difficult for her and as a result
she has to try in her own words to describe the
experience and you know how frustrating that can
be. How different the world would be if she'd had a
Sony Ericsson Z500a© with its camera and 4x zoom
to capture those minutes He Offered her in the
form of His Pale Wrist or His Muscled Thigh or His

Bony Shoulder as well as (I'm imagining) His Heart
Burning in Piety and she could have processed
those snaps she had gotten, extracted the impurities
from them, and given them back to us, to furnish
and provide, to restore us, surrendered them so
we could see, and these are all versions of *render*,
which I am having so much trouble with, because
such details as flesh and belief are tough to arrange
as metaphor.

    Thank you for your consideration, and for
reading. I have enclosed an SASE, and look forward
to hearing from you.

Sincerely,
Amy Newman

1 January

Dear Editor:

Please consider the enclosed poems for
publication. They are from my manuscript,
X = Pawn Capture, a lyrical study of chess as we
played it in my family: the first move has to take
place while everyone is thinking about something
other than chess. For my grandparents, diversion
was love, and between his rage-filled checkmates
and her play dates with saints, they braided my
teenage years spent mostly schooling and listening
and keeping the house free of insects.

When in our backyard caterpillars mastered
the flowering dogwoods, and our neighbor dispersed
them by rapping on the trees with a stick, her image
reminded my grandmother of Hortense tormenting
Germana Cousin for her presumed pilfering of
a small loaf of bread. Germana opens her dress
and her saintliness is revealed as summer flowers
tumble out in a herald of love and beauty. Here my
grandmother saw chastisement and the Holy Hand
of her Invisible Lord Partitioning The Mortals with
some tiny visuals about The Power and The Glory
but I thought if so He was really Just Sprinkling
the World with His Blossoms and Berries, and if
Germana's cottons could give way to an onrush of
flesh, abandoning its pinks and greens and holy
stamens and anthers and spilt maple leaves and

maybe even ruffles of filaments and pollen, might
it ever be under my opened dress, this mound of
petals, with my thin body lighter than bone from
what I knew? So when I looked up and the neighbor
was walking away over broken dogwood blossoms
snowing down, I wished hard for a language that
would tell you of this beautiful sight which I have
never before seen, not even on a holy card, and this
in spite of my grandmother's hissing at our neighbor
and retrieving a rake. I spent the afternoon carrying
away the remainders of Germana's undressing
and trying to find a dictionary I could bring to my
room. Because *beautiful* is a word that my workshop
class says is ineffective, that it doesn't contain how
this sight captures my attention and convinces me,
absorbs and converts me away from the yard, so that
the closest kin might be *diverting*, which the class
might find archaic, and if that's true, then I don't
know how to say that everything in the backyard
might be pretending to be lovely in order that we
can all get up in the morning.

Thank you for your consideration, and for
reading. I have enclosed an SASE, and look forward
to hearing from you.

Sincerely,
Amy Newman

Dear Editor:

Please consider the enclosed poems for
publication. They are from my manuscript,
X = Pawn Capture, a series of poems about
chess and, in particular, how the game kept my
grandfather's passions wrapped up so tightly in a
leak-proof seal that we could never locate them. I
would like to know passion, to know it in the same
way the saints know the world, which is to say in
the most pure and untouched version as it hovers
and penetrates, before it is reduced to dry ink in a
single file of letters. So that instead of crying and
running to the stable, Saint Germana's answer to
her neighbor's roughing her up is to explode out of
her aprons like a piñata of blossoms and blooms,
her fiery heart showering pollen grains and sepals
at the stigma of the world. Germana was made to
sleep in a cupboard under the stairs and returned
such unkindness with a deluge of petal, and I write
poems so I could feel as she does. In my poems I
am not unsightly and I do not hang my head when
I walk and when I open my cheerleader's uniform
to the boys who paw at it, underneath is not eczema
and scratches but wisdom and hearts of lilies and
the abundance of white notched bracts and their
tiny green true and perfect flowers unadulterated
by caterpillars.

Thank you for your consideration, and for reading. I have enclosed an SASE, and look forward to hearing from you.

Sincerely,

Amy Newman

Dear Editor:

Please consider the enclosed poems for
publication. They are from my manuscript,
$X = Pawn\ Capture$, a poetic exploration of my
grandfather's way of avoiding my grandmother's
outlook on life. My workshop teacher said good
advice for a young writer is *write what you know*,
but which is best to write about, since I know them
both, 1) the tiny burbling sound tightening in my
throat when I suppress the struggle to move my
mouth away from the boy who is kissing me, or 2)
what appears over his shoulder when I unclench
my eyes then: the flashes and flecks and the face
of Saint Theresa against a backdrop of pretty
lace, and Saint Dorothea wearing her headdress
of roses and pears, nodding and calm, their arms
practically porcelain, and their stubborn haloes like
platters as they appear on the holy cards because
they existed before artists understood how to
render perspective? What I read in the handbooks
is I should concentrate on the real, and I know
that a student will ask, if my poem diverges into
song about the basket of apples and roses from
her bridegroom's garden laid at the feet of her
tormentors, why I don't write about what is real.
But the visions I see in my shivering clenches
when I would rather not do what the boy says I

should seem as vivid as his chin jutting into my shoulder as he tries the zipper on my skirt. All that mortal wriggling pales next to the vision of Saint Marie Guyard, when she saw all her faults and human frailties in a sea of terrific blood. What if what I see is as real? This I would have to say to the class: *what if?* Nobody likes *what if*.

Thank you for your consideration, and for reading. I have enclosed an SASE, and look forward to hearing from you.

Sincerely,
Amy Newman

15 January

Dear Editor:

Please consider the enclosed poems for
publication. They are from my manuscript,
X = Pawn Capture, a lyrical study of chess as a
metaphor for childhood: my grandfather told me
nothing about either but required that I participate
in both. In the late hours of the afternoon, my
grandmother humiliated the cabbages for the
evening meal, and when we blessed the softened
food we were about to receive, I understood
how everything we own is really metaphor for
absorbing light and goodness as in the cases of
Maria Fortunata Viti, for whom the sacrament
was something to consume like a leafy green,
or Elizabeth of Schonau, so bright and unafraid
against her ecstasies.

One afternoon my grandmother had her
bridge club over to introduce the new couple
in town to the church, because she knew that
the wife was a temptress and it was the club's
intent to serve cheese crackers and crab puffs so
that the speech about His Love would go down
easily in the midst of their socializing and the
new couple would join the flock. I was delighted
by such Eucharistic intervention, a diversion of
the wafer in church. He appears all over inside
and out while you are concentrating on the soft

wafer and your throat and stomach on its caloric absorption.

But my grandmother said *the wafer is not a Holy hors d'oeuvre it is a sure piece of evidence and proof He is with us* but that's what I meant and even as I carried the trays of crab puffs with their pink interiors I decided it was right to think so because isn't grace the invisible what-ness of Thou in wherever we find It or, more to the point, where we perceive and experience the adornment of all that love? That even a silence such as what you practice with me, dear sir, I know in my heart your quiet wisdom and strength and the all-knowing all-loving hope for a fallen generation is such grace, even for this fallen sphere we maintain in gravity, this earth, this round and holy flowery mess of a bouquet tossed from Eden? Tossed with disappointment, I think, too.

Thank you for your consideration, and for reading. I have enclosed an SASE, and look forward to hearing from you.

Sincerely,
Amy Newman

Dear Editor:

Please consider the enclosed poems for
publication. They are from my manuscript,
X = Pawn Capture, a lyrical study of chess as my
grandfather played it: the first move has to be
made by someone who has not sinned. In this way
the kingdom he created could be understood as
a metaphor for family, and his fortress the dining
room table, which he occupied until dinner, when
my grandmother left off reading her calendar of
saints, and brought in the platter of cabbages, along
with her teary eyes. But I am saying too much.

As I am learning, poetry means to render as
one renders anything; a boiling down to a kind of
delicious syrup or troublesome glue, a thick liquid
magic, like the manna oil, flowing from where the
saints walked with delicate or tormented feet in life
or after, when their bodies were free of indecisions.
My grandmother reminded me of the miracle of
the oil of St. Stephen when it made a dead man
stand up and dance a kind of two-step of proof,
and everyone's eyes watered and the crowd broke
into applause, and the applause broke into doves
flapping their wings against their hearts. In Bavaria
the Oil of Saint Walburga flows out of a rock and is
captured in a souvenir chalice, so that all may be
cured of their terrible mortal leanings, such as when

the boy from the football team tries to rearrange
my blouse with his chin as I am pinned in his arms
on those nights I walk home from a meeting, and
I have been so embarrassed I can't say *no*. I have
suffocated myself with fervent blessings and he still
breathes his intentions all over me, so in my head I
carry a treasure map of Bavaria, with a little cross
for the church at Eichstadt where the relics of St.
Walburga rest. In my version of the story the stone
is a glassy green and the oils flow warm onto my
pale forehead, and my body is relaxed among the
turbulent wing beats of the grey impassioned doves.

Thank you for your consideration, and for
reading. I have enclosed an SASE, and look forward
to hearing from you.

Sincerely,
Amy Newman

1 February

Dear Editor:

Please consider the enclosed poems for publication. They are from my manuscript, $X = Pawn\ Capture$, a lyrical study of my grand-father's version of chess as a way to get back at God. He would at times declare the bishops unfit for the game and remove them from the board. If I could define why the bishop's unobstructed path across the board was a burden to my grandfather, or his passion when the wooden, intense clerics should clack this way or that, I would have a marvelous, dimensional dictionary, a book of words that would convert a priest to my poetry. And as I told my workshop class, it's difficult to convince a priest of anything when your mortal body is accumulating sin from the moment you have swallowed His Flesh and begin your molasses path back to the pew and to the handshakes and singing and intake and exhalation of breath that is this and every Sunday.

I share with those chess pieces a grasp of boundaries, although for them it is sixty-four squares and for me it is the confines of my woven clothing and my leather shoes so that although I am flesh and blood I won't make any major, life-threatening mistakes. My grandmother would not permit a dress of any fabric you might find on Cinderella or Rapunzel, such as silks or cashmeres,

georgettes or chiffons, although on every holy card
I've ever seen the saints are wearing beautiful
flowing outfits not made of tweed or corduroy, I
guarantee you. I would like a garment like Dorothy
of Caesarea, flowing and folded pink and carmine,
like the crisp apples and long-stemmed roses
she sent to her tormentors after they tortured
her for her purity and she remained, under even
those filmy fabrics, one immaculate, spotless,
reverent girl, as would I, I swear, on a stack of dull
dictionaries, even with all their understated, peevish
classifications.

Thank you for your consideration, and for
reading. I have enclosed an SASE, and look forward
to hearing from you.

Sincerely,
Amy Newman

Dear Editor:

Please consider the enclosed poems for
publication. They are from my manuscript,
$X = Pawn\ Capture$, wherein I imagine that when
the chessboard materialized, my grandfather's
spirit was hopeful and didn't begin the slow
deflation to reality until the sun made its path away
from the dining room window. Did he see in the
way light rubbed the pane and licked the grain of
the floors some kind of rare descent of a God or an
angel, or did he leave off that kind of art-making?
If I believe I'll never know, I'd have to stop revising,
for that kind of truth is the end of something my
mind wants to worry at until it's dry.

When I imagine what truth looks like to the
naked eye, I see a whitened landscape, like how the
cinema bleaches out material items for the wash of
snowy haze that is supposed to stand for dreaming,
for the blur of satori. I want to break my formal
flesh and manifest into the yes of it like some idea
of my best self, a pure cottony evaporation wherein
lies the true body of our wonderings. Isn't faith a
kind of belief that is never satisfied? Would you
agree we choose our moments? Otherwise why
would a saint see God in the form of a sewing
thimble, or an artist have so much trouble painting
the holy body of a swan as it convinces Leda? His

problem is to arrest the delicate swan's flapping
and fluttering into the impression of Divinity as
It presses Leda into a surrender of skin without
diminishing Its power into a great unwieldy comic
ovenbird. That would be doubly stressful if you
believe that God is watching as you are trying to
perceive Him enough to believe Him. It's 24/7 stress,
even on the day of rest. I don't know about you, but
my God sleeps with One Eye Open.

Thank you for your consideration, and for
reading. I have enclosed an SASE, and look forward
to hearing from you.

Sincerely,

Amy Newman

18 February

Dear Editor:

Please consider the enclosed poems for
publication. They are from my manuscript,
X = Pawn Capture, a lyrical study of chess that
now seems to have a mind of its own. For no
matter what I do, the chess games cadenced by the
accompanying sighs of my grandparents pale to
the desire I have to make them sound beautiful.
More troublesome is that I am so taken by the
emergence of the lady saints who show themselves
to me at times, although to the workshop class
these visitations would be foolish fancy and I
should write no more of them. That is a weakness
I confess only to you, in response to the promise of
privacy I observe in your absolute silence.

Asking for the details of the room in which
I negotiated the chessboard with my grandfather,
the workshop class would prefer the Victoriana of
these itemized journeys to my far-too-indistinct
wanderings. That the rug beneath the sink was of
braided dishtowels dampened by the unforgiving
tears of my grandmother is to me incidental to the
blessed hands of Catherine of Bologna outside the
window as they flutter like gray exotic birds above my
grandfather's head, gesturing in a wash of light and a
hum of crickets, and always accompanied by the scent
of the perfume of innocence that was her miracle.

Although my grandmother would have loved
to see it, when I gestured toward a similar kind of
light, rising, she slapped my hand back to my red
blood and my sinning body. Although she loved
her saints for their ecstasies, she wouldn't give
mine the time of day. One good whack with her
boned palm was enough for me and I knew when
to keep my mouth shut thereafter, but if only I
had been able to render them in their dimension
as I saw them I might have convinced her and
avoided the several afternoons of bed rest after
what she perceived as the devil in me: my utter
happiness followed by weakness and sometimes
fainting and, I admit, a little perspiration. I wish
I had a JVC Hard Drive Camcorder 0GB Everio™
G Series set up but I would have never known
where to direct the lens and at what shutter
speed, and the light would have washed out the
visions anyway. Though it is advertised as having
a clear LCD monitor to cut surface reflection
and glare even in bright sunlight, I don't think
it would stand up to the wash of radiance that
is Therese of Lisieux as she is praying above
the swirling dogwoods and my grandfather's
unperceiving body. Technology is impressive
but can it contain that kind of halo and blur of

contradiction? I could not convince anyone with a work of chaste white glare.

How maddening dimension is, based on expansion and contraction, distance and nearness, interval and contiguity, length and brevity, layer and filament, weight and support, the exterior and the interior, angles, curves, symmetry, distortion! And don't get me started on the textures of the ladies, wrapped in their filmy sheers and clusters of halo. These are the details I try to support with the blank unholy annoyance of a dictionary, a glum book disguised as enough language, within which I can't find one word to describe the look on the face of St. Anne de Beaupré, who as you know was the grandmother of Jesus Christ, when she hovers, light and elastic, by the flaking paint of the screened-in porch. Like my grandmother's, her expression is priceless, by which I mean it says more than words. But that doesn't work.

Thank you for your consideration, and for reading. I have enclosed an SASE, and look forward to hearing from you.

Sincerely,
Amy Newman

Spring

17 March

Dear Editor:

Please consider the enclosed poems for
publication. They are from my manuscript,
X = Pawn Capture. If you are familiar with chess
openings such as the Caro-Kann Defense or
the Benoni Defense, you are ahead of me, for
although my grandfather suggested I try these
attempts at early checkmate, he never explained
them. His silence may be compared unfavorably
to that silence which is the proper response to my
submissions. For I only have to exercise my faith
to know grace in our intercourse, whereas with
my grandfather it's a little harder to observe the
strength of the faithful and to believe in familial
love. Still, I cared for him amongst his tobaccos and
his soft clothing, tick-tocking his starry and willful
avoidance of me all over the dining room.

It was my grandmother I could speak to, even
if our conversations might hover around the idea
of sainthood and its challenges. For each opening
gambit in chess there is an equally ornate story I
may imagine, such as those martyrs of Saragossa—
Lupercus or Quintilian or the four Saturnii—of
which nothing is known except that they were
appallingly slain for their faith. Sometimes my
grandmother filled in the blanks in the kitchen,
sweet pies accompanying her narratives about

the martyrs' plush red hearts still beating fresh
waves of blood after death, and the horrified faces
of the tormentors who see Proof of The Way and
The Light in the flesh of the flayed skins. *Real
blood of real faith, not mere wooden pieces on black
and white squares, old man.* Where my grandfather
saw the rank and file of order and conflict, my
grandmother perceived *slashes of nonsense that
cross the afternoon with diversion*, and a *game of
secrets* compared to the truth and bloodshed of our
march toward *perfection*, which is also our *burden*.
The cherry pastry crackled and softened its plump
sacrifices into my unclean mouth and my imperfect
body within this reverie of paradise we must trudge
through, the pie tin littered with wan fruit skin
parings and the leftover crumbs of flesh. Your move.

Thank you for your consideration, and for
reading. I have enclosed an SASE, and look forward
to hearing from you.

Sincerely,
Amy Newman

21 March

Dear Editor:

Please consider the enclosed poems for
publication. They are from my manuscript,
X = Pawn Capture, a lyrical study of chess as my
grandfather invented it: the first move has to be
made when my grandmother lifted her knife to
begin chopping vegetables for the evening meal.

The sound of her chopping is hard to put
down in words, but I have tried: *restless, resigned,
determined*. The workshop says those are all clichés,
and I needn't revisit with you why we should not
use clichés. But where is the word that says the
knife understood her weariness and expressed her
will in its repetitive rush to the wood beneath the
carrots? How to say it rang my grandmother's acuity
in a pattern of messages while my grandfather
either didn't notice or made no response to her
alarms and cries, her information telegraphed
through the carrot's core in an obsolescence of her
heart's *dot dot dashes*? And you know he noticed,
and he made no response. There is more going on
in the room than details, such as the anger of the
pin-dot curtains and a rude cigar judging the air in
increments. I assure you the afternoon appeared
quiet and useful but underneath, as the scribes say,
the landscape was rising up to meet it, and when
the chessboard was put away in the sideboard,

and the bowl of softened carrots consumed, the evening became something more than what letters arranged to make sound blocks can achieve. The shaped dark that gathers beneath my window has a way of making me dream the oddest pictures in my head when my eyes are closed, in forms and manipulations and sounds. Where is the Morse code for something like that.

Thank you for your consideration, and for reading. I have enclosed an SASE, and look forward to hearing from you.

Sincerely,
Amy Newman

23 March

Dear Editor:

Please consider the enclosed poems for
publication. They are from my manuscript,
X = Pawn Capture, a lyrical study of chess as it was
played in my family: only my grandfather could
move the pieces, his hand halfway through an arc
to land on a dark square while in the kitchen my
grandmother smoothed the pages of her calendar
of saints near the square for Saint Fedelemia, who
as you know met Saint Patrick by the fountain of
Clebach before rising waiflike to her clean destiny
in a beautiful sheer cloth outfit.

My grandmother would say of me: *She is a*
young body but any unclean girl has an open door
for sin down there, is burgeoning with sin as is a
pigeon with maggots. I know that the boys who
walk me home after practice should not inspire
my heart, even if it feels like the definition of
ecstasy, all my senses suspended to that one sense,
the outer world diminished to a creak or a hiss or
stripe of noise through a door. Fedelmia died in
that language of rapture, suffering her name onto
the list of saints in a sacred branding, like the
permanent mark on the livestock, only tender and
ever charged. I am not elated but confused when a
boy pins my body to the brick of the corner posts
and his hands move like playing cards all over my

blouse. And sayeth the grandmother: like maggots
I have it.

I wish I had a sister as Fedelemia had Eithne,
as they had each other, so that when they died in
their excitements for all good reasons beneath the
fountain where they met their Patrick, to be herded,
gathering in the weight of all that innocence as
though it were a damask hem, all their hair uncoiled
and they left behind the earthly nothings, and they
could chatter and giggle and gossip as they rose. I
am a lone body with an open door that needs to be
guarded, so sayeth the grandmother.

Thank you for your consideration, and for
reading. I have enclosed an SASE, and look forward
to hearing from you.

Sincerely,
Amy Newman

28 March

Dear Editor:

Please consider the enclosed poems for publication. They are from my manuscript, *X = Pawn Capture*, a lyrical study of chess as my grandfather invented it: a game not of skill but of worry. I was to watch as the girl pieces were shamed repeatedly by the reckless kings and saved finally by the horse pieces, clopped away to the tower to wait for the judgment of a god. My grandfather would ask: *Does her soul rise?* And I was to reply: *Is there peace in her heart?* Then it would be time for dinner. But even after the spoon clinked in the last serving of potatoes I would imagine the girl's soul pierced with love if she was pure, or agony if she was taken before she could claim certainty, so that even if she was forgiven, maybe in her heart she knew that she had sinned, and it was with regret that she would watch as her body diminished in size and value in relation to the earth's size and value, and the trumpets of heaven proclaimed what's left of her A-OK. The distance between what swims before her eyes as the earth pulls away and my idea of it can only be measured with instruments I don't own. But I imagine.

Do you wonder why the earth is so tilled and sown so that one's voice can rise to the ether and dissolve there, while the soil absorbs nothing real of her: neither the sound nor the memories of the singer? I think of a deflating balloon after a town parade, by its very string pulled from the hand, like soul from body, diminishing in its airy departure. What else is there, the child thinks, as the only thing she ever owned of a bright color and a promising vista is raised and absorbed into what we presume is a kingdom of heaven. Would that be what death is: repentance ringing and resounding like an opera, when the last bit of a parade is over, and the balloon is a pin dot, and the grandfather's empty hand? I wish now I had waved at the girls and the boys from my childhood more, even though I know their miniature bodies weren't absorbed into heaven so much as molted like snakeskin for their teenage forms. But I think I will miss what we call innocence; I get the feeling we shared so much more than I had thought. And what is that gathering dark that rustles when I have to walk home from school after sundown? In that atmosphere of whirring unknowns, the threatening fields where I am alone and neither encumbered by family nor protected by family, I am the exact emotion described in the definition of the word *fear*. Thus I am for that moment clear and defined, like a revelation, a girl, almost Snow White beautiful like the books describe.

Thank you for your consideration, and for reading. I have enclosed an SASE, and look forward to hearing from you.

Sincerely,
Amy Newman

29 March

Dear Editor:

Please consider the enclosed poems for
publication. They are from my manuscript,
$X = Pawn\ Capture$, and you know all about it.
Like everything else in the world, as I deduce from
probability class and statistics and beauty, the paths
we make with our little bodies through this universe
half-real, half-jellied like summer sherbet, are small
but significant. I might make a comparison with the
pretty marks a chicken's foot makes in the scratch,
or the way a low bending pine branch will write
on spring mud, patiently, in the quiet March wind.
And that's what's going on now. The tree branch is
weighed down from the thaws, nodding and moving
the wet dirt, and I am here, writing to you, while my
grandmother stands in her boots and coat, burning
another stack of mail. I recognize the stamps on
the envelopes, of course. From this distance and
in her winter coat, I might mistake grandmother
for Euphrosyne, the saint who renounced her
possessions, dressed as a man, and for years
instructed her own father in the spiritual life, until
she revealed herself and her own father broke
into blossoms and shook with truth. But above the
burning and the smoke of the metal bin where your
replies are smoldering is the kind and shining face
of Teresa, reading the ash, and a stunning bundle of

pale green petals, and many, many, patterning birds.
I wish you could see this.

      Thank you for your consideration, and for
reading. I have enclosed an SASE, and look forward
to hearing from you.

                          Sincerely,
                         Amy Newman

30 March

Dear Editor:

Please consider the enclosed poems for publication. They are from my manuscript, *X = Pawn Capture*, a lyrical study of chess as it was played in my family: the first move is considered not an advantage, but a disadvantage, so no one begins, which makes for a darkening of the afternoon as the light through trees withdraws and the grandfather's cigar dominates, and the child believes: *I never should have come here.* I'm not yet speaking of my birth.

But when I imagine being born it is something like the Wordsworth sleep and forgetting, since I never saw a mother with grateful tears through discomfort or a father with a small cuddly toy, the kind of fetish that sets the children dreaming of a soft, pleasing life to come and chattering in class a giddy play song. I vaguely picture two faces shaped like insects, their heads traversing a car window in a drizzly afternoon and the blank and rude speedometer grinding in, my grandmother babbling about sticks and stones, and those insect heads—which I take to be distortions through the squint of child eye and the blur of rain, the rush of shame or hurt invented by families—diminishing to the smudge of windshield glass times speed, then divided by the distance of something crying.

But I think I had to invent this memory for
a short story or a paper, the subject of which was
a drive we had to take cross-country into our
imaginations. It did not require documentation or
proof of ownership. It did not require fact-checking
or buyer's remorse. Who may confirm from whence
memory derives, or to where it should propel us as
we think, and what are the terms: direction and not
velocity? Breadth and not depth? The sound of the
window closing on the choking fear, or just after?

A road is a line going forward and back, and
behind my head is an arrow pointing thusly, toward
what I picture as parents. And I am offspring, shooting
like an arrow toward my grandfather's dining table,
trussed up with the slanting afternoon ticking the
ashes from his cigar's diminishing shape. Am I right,
sir? Is this how I should represent myself on paper?
I know you won't respond, preferring the justice of
silence, the instruction of meditative thought, and I
have to agree. You know this and this and this, for you
have the instructor's edition, and are the maker of this
earth encompassed by strings of road like a ball of
yarn. Such is our doing and our undoing, our hemming
up and our disentangling. It is a kitten's story you
made from your delight that unravels in a weariness of
flaw. I will write again, though. All roads lead to you.

Thank you for your consideration, and for reading. I have enclosed an SASE, and look forward to hearing from you.

Sincerely,

Amy Newman

3 April

Dear Editor:

Oh you are indeed just, and I understand
your silences. Still, I wish for a response, some
kind of sign, even just some change in the weather,
something in the way of an answer from you.
In church as I pray, I can hear in my grandmother's
whisperings that the answer to our prayers is all
around us even if unseen to the mortal eye, since
the landscape looks the same, from when I shut
my eyes to ask for proof to the minute later, when I
open them, albeit possibly the grass is darker for a
moment. Yet I seek Your Substance in the mailman's
scuff and trumpery of his walk away without
leaving a sheet of paper bearing your response to
my queries, that bit of flesh I would so gratefully
receive for I am not worthy to, but only say the word
and I shall know. But I trust you hear me; that is my
faith. Please consider these poems for publication.
        Along the perimeters of the land my
grandmother brought into the marriage is a series
of trees that position themselves in such tall
insolence that I like to think of them as little gods
of the earth or representatives of a mythic battle.
If I wrote a book to explain these trees, I might
market it to students of history as an example of
how the world has a Presence little mortals can't
touch. By which I mean: I can't seem to write about

my defiance when my grandfather asks me to move the chess pieces, because it's not visible. Indeed I move the pieces. They trace my idea of victory and scratch out seamless truths; in the dance of my queen and my horse and my pawn, I write notes and letters and notions and sayings and the grandfather grumbles and the grandmother stirs. As the afternoon decides what kind of evening to become, the grandmother humiliates the rhubarb into a courteous shape, and the carrots, too, surrender to their destiny, but neither she nor grandfather know.

But, dear Editor, You know. That is my secret to You in my bowed head. With each sweep of the chess pieces I offer myself among the other flawed human rooks and pawns, and the patterns You sent out in those green sentinels. You know my stubbornness is a silly silhouette, my tiny mortal weakness in the shadows Your Trees cast. That's all I need to say for now. Please don't overlook me.

Thank you for your consideration, and for reading. I have enclosed an SASE, and look forward to hearing from you.

Sincerely,
Amy Newman

5 April

Dear Editor:

And you know being a cheerleader was an extracurricular gift, an agreement between the school spirit team and something in myself, to be a part of a larger secular experience, so sayeth the grandparents, and who am I to disagree? I can jump and cheer and shake the poms as do the others. I didn't anticipate the fumbling boys or the silence of petulant girls, but I am familiar with the feeling of difference: the sweater a little bulky, the felt of my skirt never falling as sharp as the others. And the boy who walks with me into the field after practice should be forgiven for his own stunned stares and the tears and the surprise. He was covered with boils on both hands, and the coach was talking about benching him so he was upset anyway, and when I touched the wounds as he tried to push apart the different aspects of my clothing— when I felt for his hands as he separated the agreement between my sweater and my t-shirt, the chapters written in the pleats of my skirt and the underneath—there was that familiar, comfortable heat and that lush, respectful music, and that light I tried to write about in workshop, the light that tells me how much language lets me down, the light for which every single adjective fails, fails, fails. I am still trying.

But to get to the point: his hands clear now, soft and clean, and his face shiny, startled, and the mouth open as I stood with him among the falling blooms and the wind blowing perfumes. First the birds stopped their chatter, and then began again that lovely twirring, beneath which we both stared at his hands as he picked up a pie pumpkin, stepped back a little, and tossed it through the far maples. In the autumn gold arc the vegetable pronounced, I saw the outline of everything, pulled back like a camera angle, only more so. There was nothing to preserve it except my mind and this stiff, unwavering language, this combination of seeing and thinking. His hands were lovely, and he held them for a minute clasped. Then off he ran.

It was a pretty gift, to be able to do it for him, and to take into myself his suffering, and to ask nothing more, but to receive. These are such small things we all do, playing football, walking to school, living with one's grandparents, seeing the face of Teresa in the wind, figuring geometry, crying at books, hearing arguments, wondering, waiting, believing, disbelieving: such small patterns the human makes, scratches, in each detail, immensity, and in every pattern, sincerity, and in so many dimensions at once. That's the way I would describe that light for which there aren't any words, and the way it was still there when I walked home alone, the boy having run off. Alone except for the knowing, and that's when I started writing to you.

Thank you for your consideration, and for reading. I have enclosed an SASE, and look forward to hearing from you.

Sincerely,
Amy Newman

11 April

Dear Editor:

Please consider the enclosed poems for
publication. They are from my manuscript,
X = Pawn Capture, poems I'm trying to write about
how, when a family prays together with bowed
heads, there might be a granddaughter noticing
how the dust motes in the afternoon sun rays
drift in a kind of suspension through the stained
yellow windows, hover weightless, like the little
bronze flecks of proteins and irons that float on
the surface of the pond water until she waggles
a blade of grass and they float down in the most
pacific of increments, as the muscular orange fish
below, having waited in swim-still forms, behave
in a patience which can't be measured outside of
the waters, scissor here and there and break the
surface only to be satisfied by the bit on the tongue
as a sign, and then swim back down again, satisfied
amongst the rushes.

Having gone so far out from where I should
have been in my prayer, I wonder if whoever
releases the mercy in downward flecks and
bits through the terra inconceivable notices my
daydreaming and places the manna elsewhere
on purpose because I have been so tiresome, in
which case I apologize for getting off the subject.
I meant to tell you about the overlooked Saint

Gemma Galgani, whom nobody believed, even with her stigmata and her cures, and who, without her own faith, might have looked down and thought of herself as the product of so many paper cuts, all for naught. From trying so hard. And not much floating down kindly to her, you understand. It can be frustrating to be this way. The waiting is what I mean.

Thank you for your consideration, and for reading. I have enclosed an SASE, and look forward to hearing from you.

Sincerely,
Amy Newman

17 April

Dear Editor:

Please consider the enclosed poems for
publication. They are from my manuscript,
X = Pawn Capture, a lyrical exploration that tries
to be about everything and to contain everything,
but fails like the periodic table of the elements or
the categories of physics. I can find you in neither,
but both are lovely to study when the footsteps of
a grandfather so tired of it all insinuate themselves
into any given room. Let my words be acceptable
to you, to magnify and be magnified, in order that
we may one day be fully aware of whatever gift has
been sent our way, even though it's obvious to me
there isn't anything there to see, to actually see.
The dimension is private. My longing is the deer's
longing, which I can place not under Velocity or
Torque but maybe Pressure, Reflection, or Relativity.
You can see I'm thinking of Saint Philomena,
the saint of having been forgotten, who was
discovered as bones only, and later catalogued
without the blood-soaked and blossoming-from-
torment virginity and martyrdom histories that are
my grandmother's bedtime stories. On the calendar
it says Philomena was effectively forgotten since
there is nothing to know. She should have been the
saint of Momentum and Light, against desperate
causes, against lost causes, against everything that

seems forgotten, as she moved through the ether and made soft impressions and threw grass stems at her brother or, if she had no brother, she at least looked at water in a stream and noticed how it rushed or, if there was not a stream, she maybe had a horse. She existed, she had dimension, and you'll forgive me, it doesn't seem fair she should be forgotten, having come all that way to be and put so much of herself into a little slip of wandering. Of what consequence are the elements of which she is made as they passed by the elements of which the tree is made if she only left little marks of nothing on nothing, all that rotation of Field and Force and Image and Mass? And not turned into a shower of roses or golden twisted cables of burning holy love or a field of almond blossoms. Did she look forward to hearing from you? She sent out her breath into the air and I think that is enough to write a history, albeit unseen. It is not enough to come to nothing. So I see her.

On her holy card Philomena is always breathtaking, impossible to forget, represented by a combination of anchors and arrows, the anchor I guess because she was weighed down by the sobering fact of being a human girl, and I'll say for her, since she has no history, that arrows are

a metaphor for praying, for the rising volley of
expectation and belief propelled through currents,
and thank goodness when the arrows fell, if they
fell, it was out of her view. All proposals whatever
the crest, should seem to remain ever buoyant.
Here is mine, as the earth shifts its properties to
fit inside my head, and the heavens flutter and
everything should be trumpeting glorious, and we'll
all have a good cry: please consider these poems for
publication.

  This petition is a good example of what I mean.
Belief requires my sending my postage stamp crest
and white vanes, those agitations of my heart's
velocity, forcefully into the unseen, and there it all
levitates, and nothing coming back.

Sincerely,
Amy Newman

24 April

Dear Editor:

I have been thinking about significance, the
path to becoming significant. That the saints merit
their sweet, white, isolated, salt-like perfection,
and wander amongst us in their beauty, and
sweeten the various layers of air and earth and
my own mind, is universally understood. But how
does it happen?

For instance, Catherine of Alexandria: In my
head I mark a tiny point to represent her birth, and
then a series of dots along a parabola to indicate her
conversion, the debates, the subsequent scourging
and imprisonment. I put a tiny star at the moment
when she gently touched the stretching wheel
she was sentenced to die on, that wheel simply
collapsing like it was melting into the ground at her
touch. Another star where her body is carried off
by angels, the everything following the fact of her
beatitude. On what dot should I mark the moment
she goes from being merely human? Was it when
she lifted little petals to the mouths of birds as a
child? I imagine the vertex intersecting in a holy
glowing ivory indicator, the whole axis of the thing
deepening directly from this intersection like when
I use a woodburner to mark the chicken crates, or
when something in a movie is so significant that the
camera does a triple take: look, look. Look.

Who introduces the name of the poor girl
who so lovingly served, who gets to nominate the
saints, I wonder? Who notices the true absolute
and fervent devotion almost as if she held the only
last ticket to knowing, not to mention passion and
belief, consolation and suffering—who notices
her? Behold and see. Margaret of Cortona received
messages from heaven in her ecstasies. This is my
confession. The saints aren't metaphors, and visions
aren't avoidable. I don't mind. Teresa wanders the
halls in the breeze sometimes, in this mansion
of being where I try to put into these words my
attempts of knowing. Like my grandfather's cigars,
you either like them or you don't, and if you don't,
you can always go outside by the ash can where
grandmother is burning the letters. In the rising
grays of smoke and carbons, and above the familiar
pages, are images, ideas, doves, blessings, bits
whirling, char, fibers, patterns, visions among the
broken tree limbs when I look up, and clouds, dirt,
rain, air, fire: the ends and beginnings of thought. I
wish you could see this.

Thank you for your consideration, and for
reading. Forgive my trespasses.

Sincerely,
Amy Newman

Acknowledgments

I am grateful to the editors of the following publications where "Dear Editor" poems first appeared, some in slightly different form: *Absent Magazine, Center, Colorado Review, DIAGRAM, The Georgia Review, Hotel Amerika, The Laurel Review, Mid-American Review, /nor:, Seneca Review, Sentence,* and *West Branch.*

"Dear Editor 10 October" appears in *An Introduction to the Prose Poem,* published by Firewheel Editions. "Dear Editor 30 October," "Dear Editor 19 November," and "Dear Editor 18 January" appear in *The Rose Metal Press Field Guide to Prose Poetry: Contemporary Poets in Discussion and Practice.*

This book is dedicated to Joe Bonomo.

About the Author

Amy Newman is the author of the poetry collections *Order, or Disorder*; *Camera Lyrica*; and *fall*. Her poems and essays have appeared in numerous journals, including *Denver Quarterly*, *The Georgia Review*, *The Gettysburg Review*, *Hotel Amerika*, *The Kenyon Review*, *Narrative*, and *Ploughshares*; and in *The Iowa Anthology of New American Poetries*, *An Introduction to the Prose Poem*, and *The Rose Metal Press Field Guide to Prose Poetry*. She is the founding editor of *Ancora Imparo: A Journal of Arts, Process, and Remnant*, and Presidential Research Professor at Northern Illinois University.

The Lexi Rudnitsky
Editor's Choice Award

The Lexi Rudnitsky Editor's Choice Award is a collaboration between Persea Books and The Lexi Rudnitsky Poetry Project. It sponsors the annual publication of a poetry collection by an American who has published at least one previous full-length book of poems.

Lexi Rudnitsky (1972–2005) grew up outside of Boston, and studied at Brown University and Columbia University. Her own poems exhibit both a playful love of language and a fierce conscience. Her writing appeared in *The Antioch Review, Columbia: A Journal of Literature and Art, The Nation, The New Yorker, The Paris Review, Pequod,* and *The Western Humanities Review.* In 2004, she won the Milton Kessler Memorial Prize for Poetry from *Harpur Palate.*

Lexi died suddenly in 2005, just months after the birth of her first child and the acceptance for publication of her first book of poems, *A Doorless Knocking into Night* (Mid-List Press, 2006). The Lexi Rudnitsky First Book Prize in Poetry and the Lexi Rudnitsky Editor's Choice Award were created to memorialize Lexi and to promote the type of poet and poetry in which she so spiritedly believed.